The dressing up

Story written by Gill Munton
Illustrated by Tim Archbold

Speed Sounds

Consonants   *Ask children to say the sounds.*

f	l	m	n	r	s	v	z	sh	(th)	(ng)
ff	(ll)		nn	rr	ss	ve	zz			(nk)
	le		kn				s			

b	c	d	g	h	j	p	qu	t	w	x	y	(ch)
bb	k	dd	gg			(pp)		(tt)	wh			tch
	(ck)											

Each box contains one sound but sometimes more than one grapheme.
*Focus graphemes for this story are **circled**.*

Vowels

Ask children to say the sounds in and out of order.

a	e ea	i	o	u	ay	ee y	igh	ow
at	hen	in	on	up	day	see	high	blow

oo	oo	ar	or	air	ir	ou	oy
zoo	look	car	for	fair	whirl	shout	boy

Story Green Words

Ask children to read the words first in Fred Talk and then say the word.

Miss Fox   Jack Nap   Kim Cox   Meg   wig

chest   kilt   mask

Ask children to say the syllables and then read the whole word.

flip|flops   hot|pants   spott|y   flapp|y

Red Words

all	me	you	said
the	be	her	he
call	want	I've	to
no	my	your	we

The dressing up box

"Is that you?" said Miss Fox.

"Is that you, Jack Nap,
in the pink wig and the cap,
and the hotpants and the vest,
with S on the chest?"

"Is that you?" said Miss Fox.

"Is that you, Kim Cox,

in the long spotty socks,

and the red bat top,

and the flappy flipflops?"

"Meg, is that you, can I ask,

in the kilt and the mask,

and the big black hat ...

Is that you, in all that?"

"Yes, it's me, Jack Nap,

in the pink wig and the cap."

"Yes, it's me, Kim Cox,
in the long spotty socks."

"Yes, it's me!"

Questions to talk about

Ask children to TTYP for each question using 'Fastest finger' (FF) or 'Have a think' (HaT).

p.9 (FF) What four things has Jack put on?

p.10 (FF) What three things has Kim put on?

p.11 (FF) What three things has Meg put on?